SCHOLASTIC discover more™

sharks

By David Burnie

2

Know your sharks

You've been shark tracking all summer—can you recognize these sharks?

Tip

Hunt in your print and digital books for matching shark shapes!

1 Ⓐ Whale shark Ⓑ Leopard shark

2 Ⓐ Angel shark Ⓑ Mako shark

3 Ⓐ Basking shark Ⓑ Whale shark

4 Ⓐ Saw shark Ⓑ Hammerhead shark

5 Ⓐ Frilled shark Ⓑ Wobbegong shark

6 Ⓐ Great white shark Ⓑ Bull shark

Take fun shark quizzes—how much do you know about the world's most famous fish?

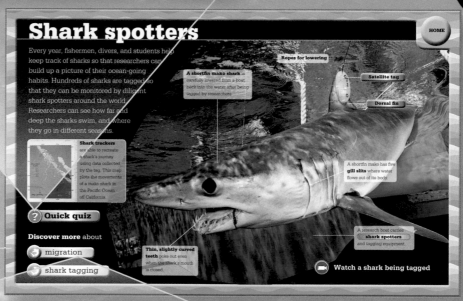

Shark spotters

HOME

Every year, fishermen, divers, and students help keep track of sharks so that researchers can build up a picture of their ocean-going habits. Hundreds of sharks are tagged so that they can be monitored by diligent shark spotters around the world. Researchers can see how far and deep the sharks swim, and where they go in different seasons.

Shark trackers are able to recreate a shark's journey using data collected by the tag. This map plots the movements of a make shark in the Pacific Ocean off California.

? **Quick quiz**

Discover more about

migration

shark tagging

Ropes for lowering

A shortfin mako shark is carefully lowered from a boat back into the water after being tagged by researchers

Satellite tag

Dorsal fin

A shortfin mako has five **gill slits** where water flows out of its body

A research boat carries **shark spotters** and tagging equipment.

Thin, slightly curved teeth poke out even when the shark's mouth is closed.

📹 Watch a shark being tagged

Meet cool and crazy shark people, from marine biologists to filmmakers to shark taggers.

more

migration

Most sharks do not stay in the same area all year round. Divers and fishermen have found that huge whale sharks head to different parts of the Indian Ocean in spring and fall, and hundreds of hammerhead sharks travel together in search of cooler waters each summer. Many sharks, like other animals, have patterns of places that they visit at different times of the year, known as migration routes. Some creatures cannot survive in cold weather, so they migrate, or travel, to warmer places. Many animals migrate in search of a better supply of food, others migrate to find somewhere to give birth. Some sharks travel thousands of miles across the ocean; others just swim farther around the coast.

In 62 days, a hammerhead shark swam

745 miles (1,200 km)

from Florida to the coast of New Jersey

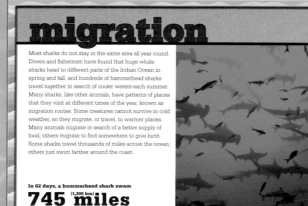

Read in-depth information about sharks and ocean life.

It's simple to get your digital book. Go to the website (see left), enter the code, and download the book. Make sure you open it using Adobe Reader.

Consultant: Kim Dennis-Bryan, PhD
Literacy Consultant: Barbara Russ,
21st Century Community Learning Center
Director for Winooski (Vermont) School District
Editor: Slaney Begley
Designers: Clare Joyce, Tory Gordon-Harris
Art Director: Bryn Walls
Managing Editor: Miranda Smith
Managing Production Editor:
Stephanie Engel
US Editor: Esther Lin
Cover Designer: Neal Cobourne
DTP: John Goldsmid
Digital Photography Editor: Stephen Chin
Visual Content Project Manager:
Diane Allford-Trotman
**Executive Director of Photography,
Scholastic:** Steve Diamond

Library of Congress Cataloging-in-Publication
Data Available

ISBN 978-0-545-49561-5

10 9 8 7 6 5 4 3 2 1   13 14 15 16 17

Printed in Singapore   46
First edition, March 2013

Scholastic is constantly working to lessen the
environmental impact of our manufacturing
processes. To view our industry-leading
paper procurement policy, visit
www.scholastic.com/paperpolicy.

Contents

All about sharks

Around the world

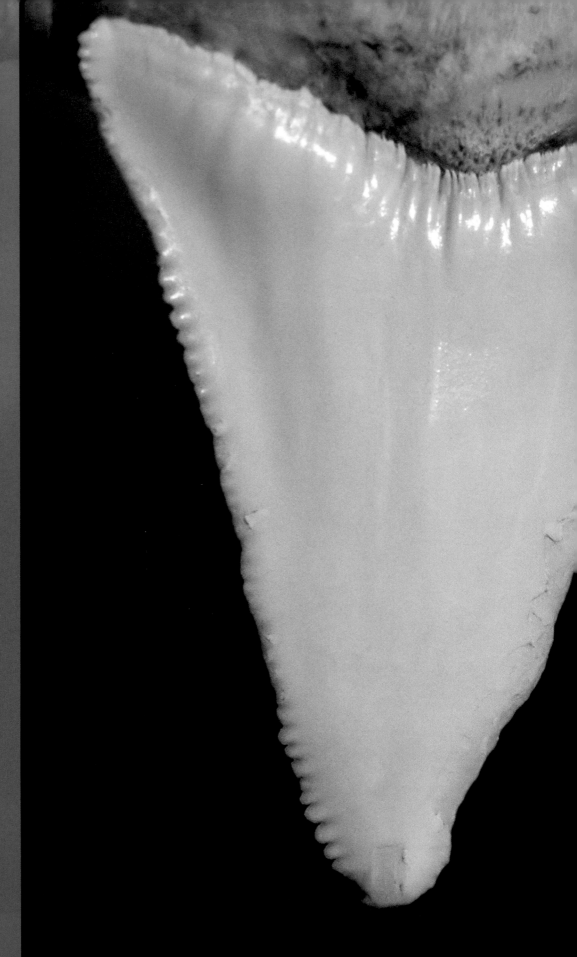

All about sharks

Imagine a shark. Are you thinking . . . razor-sharp teeth? Streamlined body? Menacing fins? You got it! There are over 400 kinds of shark, all different, and all part of a group that has dominated the oceans for millions of years.

What is a shark?

Sharks are powerful, predatory fish that have been around, virtually unchanged, for millions of years. They are sleek and streamlined, have super senses, and grow new teeth nonstop.

Often all you will see of a shark above water is its front dorsal fin.

Anatomy of a shark

Many sharks, like this great white, have jaws slung beneath their snouts. A shark's skeleton is not made of heavy bone. Instead, it is made of a lighter, elastic material called cartilage.

The eyeball rolls back for protection when the shark attacks prey.

A shark "breathes" by taking oxygen from water. Used water exits the shark's body through gill slits on both sides of its head.

A pair of pectoral (chest) fins is used for steering and for keeping the shark level.

Many sharks have big, oily livers that act as built-in

Under threat

⚠️

People have killed too many sharks for food, and now some species are endangered. Look through the book for the yellow signs to see which ones they are.

Fishermen threw the body of this smooth hammerhead overboard.

The snout contains special electrical organs for finding unseen prey.

Weird shapes

Bottom-dwelling sharks are very different from ones that prowl the open sea. Many have flat bodies. Some have saw-shaped snouts that they use to slash prey.

Shark relatives

Sharks aren't the only fish that have skeletons made of cartilage—spookfish and rays do, too. Find out more on pages 12–13.

eagle ray

Pacific spookfish

Shark lineup

There are more than 400 species, or kinds, of shark, divided into 8 main orders, or groups. On average, a new species of shark or shark relative is discovered every two weeks.

tropical saw shark

spiny dogfish

prickly dogfish

Dogfish

NUMBER OF SPECIES: 119

EXAMPLE: Spiny dogfish

FUN FACT: The spiny dogfish is one of the most common species of shark.

Saw sharks

NUMBER OF SPECIES: 8

EXAMPLE: Tropical saw shark

FUN FACT: A saw shark's snout can be up to a third of its total length. That's some nose!

whale shark

eastern angel shark

Angel sharks

NUMBER OF SPECIES: 19

EXAMPLE: Eastern angel shark

FUN FACT: Angel sharks will often wait a week for the right meal to come along.

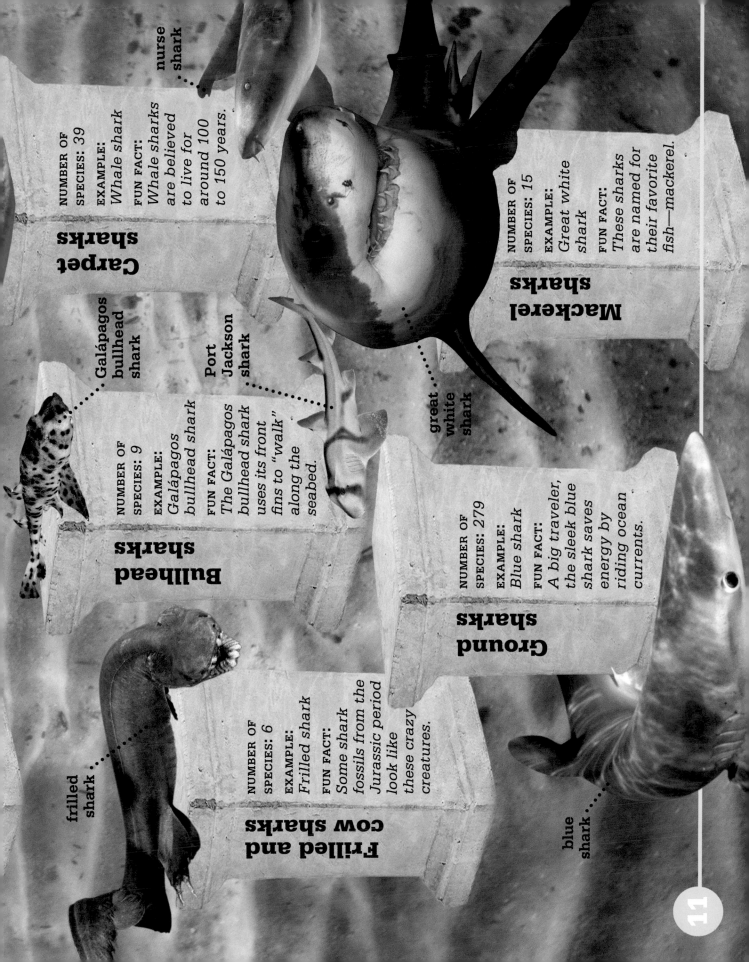

Carpet sharks

NUMBER OF SPECIES: 39

EXAMPLE: Whale shark

FUN FACT: Whale sharks are believed to live for around 100 to 150 years.

nurse shark

Mackerel sharks

NUMBER OF SPECIES: 15

EXAMPLE: Great white shark

FUN FACT: These sharks are named for their favorite fish—mackerel.

great white shark

Bullhead sharks

NUMBER OF SPECIES: 9

EXAMPLE: Galápagos bullhead shark

FUN FACT: The Galápagos bullhead shark uses its front fins to "walk" along the seabed.

Galápagos bullhead shark

Port Jackson shark

Ground sharks

NUMBER OF SPECIES: 279

EXAMPLE: Blue shark

FUN FACT: A big traveler, the sleek blue shark saves energy by riding ocean currents.

blue shark

Frilled and cow sharks

NUMBER OF SPECIES: 6

EXAMPLE: Frilled shark

FUN FACT: Some shark fossils from the Jurassic period look like these crazy creatures.

frilled shark

Close relatives

Sharks have plenty of relatives that swim, glide, or shuffle through the seas. But being "in the family" doesn't guarantee safety—some of these fish are also favorite shark prey.

Chimaeras
Chimaeras, also known as spookfish or rabbitfish, live close to the seabed. Instead of sharp teeth, they have flat plates for crushing hard-shelled food.

Ogilby's ghost shark

elephant fish

rabbitfish

spotted ratfish

Pacific spookfish

ghost shark

manta ray

leopard whip ray

Tasmanian numbfish

spiny butterfly ray

blue-spotted fantail ray

thornback skate

spotted stingaree

eastern shovelnose ray

common eagle ray

short-tail torpedo ray

bowmouth guitarfish

Skates and rays

These fish have broad pectoral (chest) fins that work like wings. Most live on the seafloor, but the manta "flies" through open sea.

Sydney skate

peacock skate

Ancient fish

Sharks have been around for at least 420 million years. That's well before there were insects, flowers, or dinosaurs on Earth, and over 419 million years before humans.

Stethacanthus

Wonders of the ancient world

Over millions of years, the oceans have been home to some strange and fearsome sharks that are now extinct.

This small shark had a flat-topped fin on its back that looked like an ironing board.

Jellyfish have lived in the oceans for over 500 million years. They've been around for even longer than sharks have.

The color of a shark-tooth fossil depends on where

Megalodon

An enormous and powerful predator, Megalodon *was* up to 65 feet (20 m) long.

Cladoselache— one of the first sharks—lived 400 million years ago.

Cladoselache

This shark is known only from fossils of its bizarre teeth, which grew in spiral coils.

Helicoprion

Megatooth

Megalodon's teeth were up to 7 inches (18 cm) long—that's as big as a human hand.

the tooth was buried.

On the move

Imagine having to swim all the time. If you stop, you drown. That's what life is like for some kinds of shark. They swim even in their sleep.

Tail power

A lemon shark swishes its powerful tail fin back and forth to move forward. Its other fins keep it on a stable course.

lemon
shark .....

The need for speed

Sharks need to be fast to grab their food out in the open sea. Some kinds can swim at 40 mph (65 kph)—that's fast enough to catch birds and dolphins.

Rough stuff

A shark's skin is covered with sharp scales. These streamline the shark and soften the sounds it makes as it stalks prey.

yummy
tern ...

tasty
penguin ....

tender
. dolphin

Sharks can't stop quickly, and **they can't**

Breathing

As a shark swims, water flows through its mouth and over its gills, which collect oxygen for it to breathe. Then the water flows back out through gill slits on either side of its head.

Find out more about shark tails on pages 40–41.

Its tail fin can change the shark's direction by changing the angle of its body.

A lemon shark has a streamlined body that glides easily through the water.

Attack from below   Stealth + speed = certain death!

1 Easy prey
A seal relaxes on the ocean surface, happily unaware of any danger.

2 Hunting shark
A great white strikes the seal from below at 25 mph (40 kph).

3 Breaching
The shark flies through the air, the seal clamped in its deadly jaws.

swim backward.

Sensing prey

Sharks have the same senses that we do, including an amazing sense of smell. But they also have another sense—they can detect the electrical fields around their prey.

Sight 82 ft. (25 m)

Electricity 3 ft. (1 m)

Vibrations 330 ft. (100 m)

Hearing 1 mi. (1.5 km)

Smell 3 mi. (5 km)

Perfect predator

Sharks are excellent at locating prey. Some can see in the dark better than a cat can, and they can smell 10,000 times better than a human can. Almost nothing is safe in the ocean!

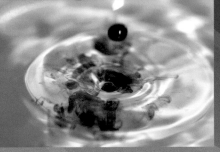

Smell
Sharks can smell a drop of blood in an area the size of an Olympic pool.

Hearing
A shark can hear splashing sounds with ears inside its head.

One-seventh of a great white shark's brain is devoted

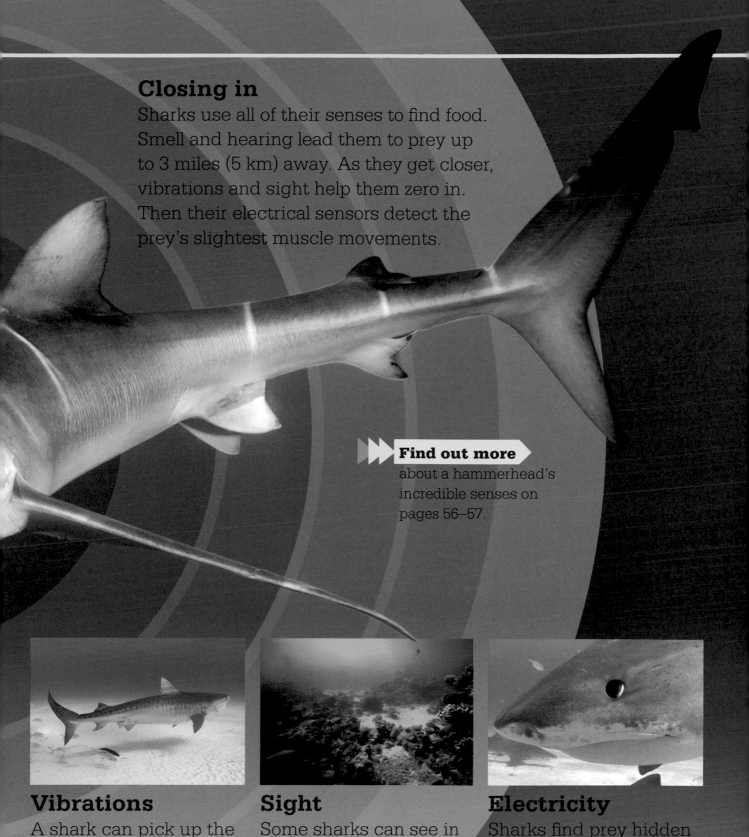

Closing in

Sharks use all of their senses to find food. Smell and hearing lead them to prey up to 3 miles (5 km) away. As they get closer, vibrations and sight help them zero in. Then their electrical sensors detect the prey's slightest muscle movements.

▶▶▶ **Find out more** ▶
about a hammerhead's incredible senses on pages 56–57.

Vibrations
A shark can pick up the vibrations made by prey thrashing in the water.

Sight
Some sharks can see in dim light, which allows them to hunt at night.

Electricity
Sharks find prey hidden in sand by detecting the electricity they emit.

to helping its sense of smell.

Eating machines

Imagine being crunched by a great white's 3-inch-long (7.5 cm) teeth. Sharks are highly developed eating machines that munch on a huge range of prey.

great white shark

Tactics of a kill

Some sharks herd a school of fish into a "bait ball." The shark then rushes through the center of the ball to grab its food.

copper shark ....

Jaws!

Unlike most animals, sharks can move their top and bottom jaws independently. This gives their bites a machinelike precision when they attack.

A great white has a bite force of around 2 tons—that's about 20 times stronger than a human's bite.

Deadly teeth

Most shark teeth are shaped to slice and tear. Sharks that feed on shellfish have teeth shaped for crushing.

great white shark jaw

prickly dogfish jaw

Like our own teeth, sharks' teeth are covered in hard enamel.

A mighty gulp

Sharks can't chew their food. Instead, they bite off big pieces and swallow them whole.

A basking shark filters 395,000 gallons (1.5 million L)

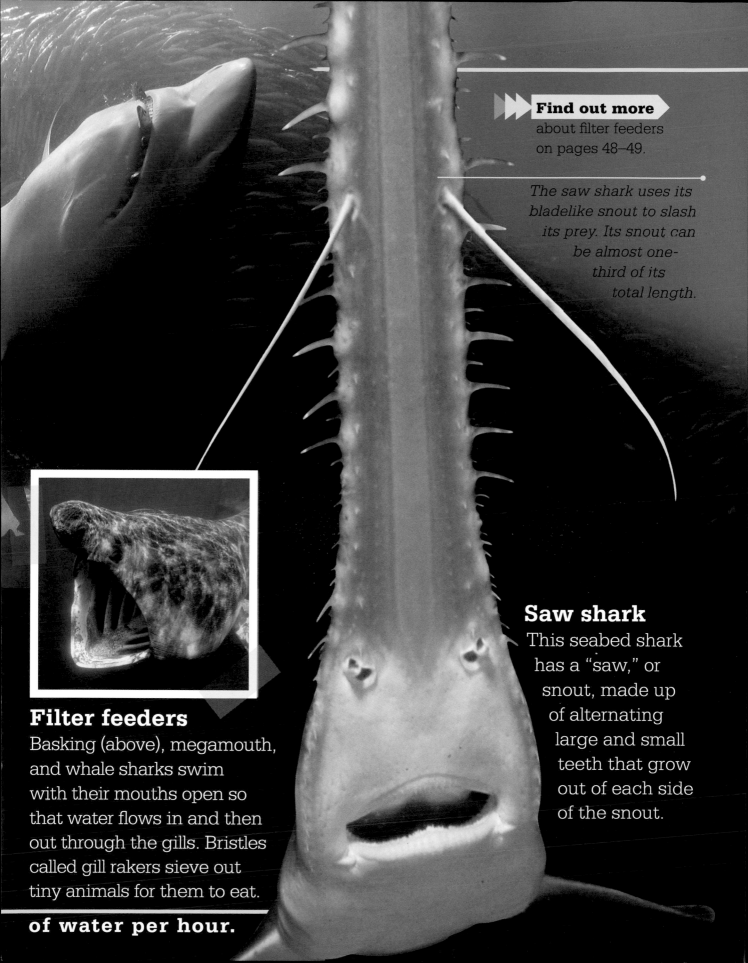

▶▶▶ **Find out more** about filter feeders on pages 48–49.

The saw shark uses its bladelike snout to slash its prey. Its snout can be almost one-third of its total length.

Saw shark
This seabed shark has a "saw," or snout, made up of alternating large and small teeth that grow out of each side of the snout.

Filter feeders
Basking (above), megamouth, and whale sharks swim with their mouths open so that water flows in and then out through the gills. Bristles called gill rakers sieve out tiny animals for them to eat.

of water per hour.

Feeding frenzy

There's a reason why sharks, such as these lemon sharks, usually eat alone. If multiple sharks try to attack the same prey, the sharks may go crazy, biting furiously at anything in their way—even one another.

Shark babies

Most shark babies, called pups, grow inside their mothers, but some hatch from eggs laid on the ocean floor.

New life

A lemon shark pup gets food from its mother as it grows inside her for 10–12 months. Lemon sharks can give birth to as many as 17 pups at one time.

When pups are born, they are already able to swim and hunt.

Incredible eggs

Some sharks, such as the cloudy cat shark, lay eggs in strangely shaped cases on the ocean floor.

A whale shark was found to be pregnant with a record

The leathery egg cases are 2 inches (5.5 cm) long. The pups may hatch in 7–9 months.

Case notes Watch a swell shark grow.

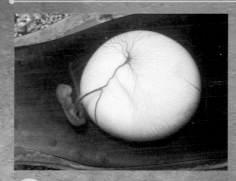

1 First food
Inside its egg case on the ocean floor, a shark embryo feeds on yolk.

2 Speedy exit
When fully grown, the shark wriggles free of its case and swims away.

Born killers
Some sharks, like the spiny dogfish, hatch from eggs while still inside their mothers. For food, they eat their weaker brothers and sisters. Then they are born.

Spiny dogfish embryos have teeth.

yolk sac of food ....

300 embryos—that's one mega-mom!

Hall of fame

There are giant ones, small ones, superspeedy ones, and very deadly ones. Meet some of the record holders of the shark world.

LONGEST TAIL
The tail fin of the thresher shark can be up to 10 ft. (3 m) long—that's about the same length as its body.

SMALLEST
At under 9 in. (22 cm) long, the pygmy shark is one of the tiniest known sharks.

LARGEST
Whale sharks, the world's largest living fish, can be up to 59 ft. (18 m) long and weigh over 22 tons— that's more than three male African elephants.

DEADLIEST
The three sharks most dangerous to humans are great white, tiger, and bull sharks (below).

WORST TABLE MANNERS
The cookie-cutter shark bites cookie-shaped chunks of flesh from its prey.

LARGEST PREDATOR
The great white—20 ft. (6 m) long and over 2 tons in weight—is the world's largest predatory fish.

UGLIEST
With its weird, beaklike snout and pink body, the goblin shark won't win any beauty contests!

FASTEST
Able to reach speeds of 40 mph (65 kph) in short bursts, the shortfin mako is the fastest shark.

MOST POISONOUS
The flesh of the Greenland shark is poisonous to humans unless it is washed thoroughly.

Around the **World**

Every part of the ocean — from coastal shallows to coral reefs to open sea — is home to hungry sharks seeking prey. Some hide on the seafloor, but others are tireless travelers, migrating across whole oceans to feed and breed.

At sea

The world's biggest sharks wander the oceans in an endless quest for food. Some filter feed. Others use their power and speed to catch fish, seals, and birds in open water.

oceanic whitetip shark

dusky shark

basking shark

crocodile shark

silky shark

pelagic thresher shark

shortfin mako shark

tiger shark

whale shark

cookie-cutter shark

great white shark

blue shark

porbeagle shark

goblin shark

Great white

The world's largest predatory fish is in danger. Even its huge muscles and powerful jaws are no match for the lines and nets of trophy hunters. Year after year, great whites are caught and killed.

Not just white

The great white is gray on top and white beneath. This coloring is known as countershading.

A great white's shading hides it when it swims above its prey.

GREAT WHITE SHARK
Carcharodon carcharias
ORDER
Mackerel sharks
BODY LENGTH
20 feet (6 m)
HABITAT

Range of shark

RISK TO HUMANS

⚠️

You are more likely to be killed by a bee than by

Movie villain

In 1975, Steven Spielberg's film *Jaws* portrayed the great white shark as a man-eating machine. In response, people started killing them for sport.

People were terrified of sharks after seeing the movie Jaws.

The unknown great white

Despite being one of the most famous creatures on the planet, the great white is full of surprises. Take a look at some of its lesser-known characteristics.

Curious
A great white will often spy-hop, or pop its head out of the water, to see what's going on.

Intelligent
Like us, great whites learn as they grow. Young sharks aren't as good at hunting as older sharks are.

Careful
Great whites avoid fights. They tail slap the water—the one with the biggest splash is top shark!

Sociable
Sharks check one another out. Great whites sometimes socialize in pairs or small groups.

a great white shark.

Deadly leap

Off the coast of South Africa, a 3,000-pound (1,400 kg) great white bursts out of the water with the force of a speeding car. Its target—a young fur seal—is thrown 10 feet (3 m) in the air by the shark's unsuccessful strike, and will eventually end up in its jaws.

Girl has lucky escape from shark attack

Watch out!

In October 2003, 13-year-old Bethany Hamilton and her friends the Blanchards were surfing off Kauai, an island in Hawaii. It was sunny and warm, and turtles were loafing in the early morning surf. Bethany had ridden one breaker and was paddling out to reach the next when a tiger shark attacked her, tearing off her left arm at

the shoulder. As Bethany went into shock, the Blanchards rushed her back to the shore. By the time she reached the hospital, she had lost half of the blood in her body.

Bethany's treatment involved several major operations, but she made a full recovery. Despite her injuries, she began surfing again after just one

Most attacks on surfers and swimmers in Hawaii are carried out by tiger sharks (see pages 38–39).

Turtle or surfer?

Great white and tiger sharks may not mean to attack humans. From below, surfers look like turtles, which these sharks like to eat.

Turtle

Surfer

month, training herself to paddle with a single arm. Four years later, Bethany turned professional. She is now one of the top 50 female surfers in the whole world.

Bethany was presented with a special Courage Award at the 2004 Teen Choice Awards.

TYPES OF ATTACK

Shark attacks on humans are rare. When sharks do attack, they use different techniques.

1 Hit and run

The shark takes a test bite, then swims away. Sharks don't usually eat humans— we're too bony.

2 Bump and bite

The shark circles before nudging its victim and taking a bite. This is a more dangerous kind of attack.

3 Sneak attack

The shark takes one bite, and may come back for a second helping.

Tiger

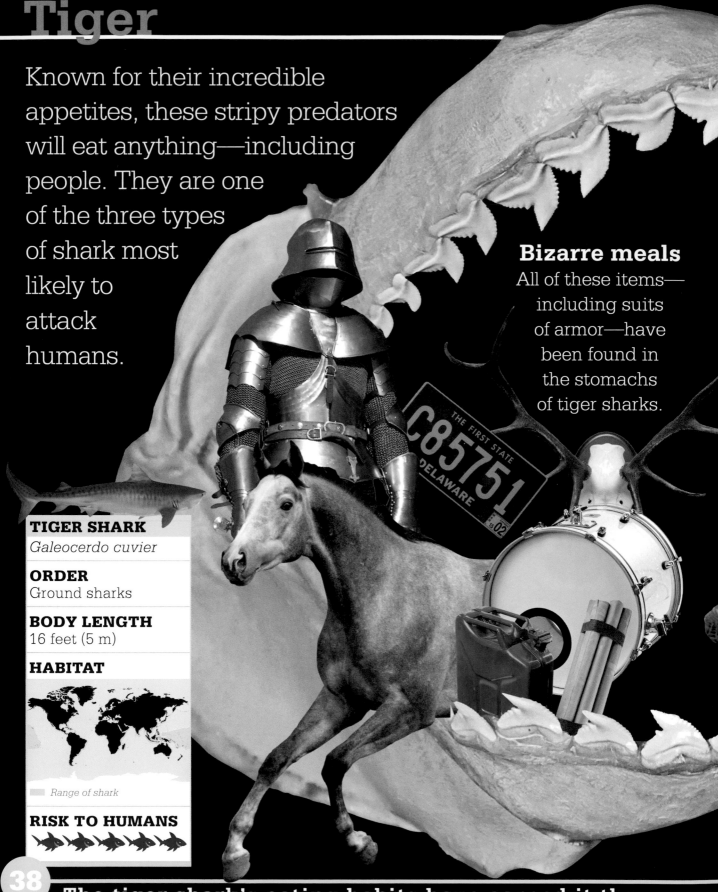

Known for their incredible appetites, these stripy predators will eat anything—including people. They are one of the three types of shark most likely to attack humans.

Bizarre meals
All of these items—including suits of armor—have been found in the stomachs of tiger sharks.

TIGER SHARK
Galeocerdo cuvier

ORDER
Ground sharks

BODY LENGTH
16 feet (5 m)

HABITAT

Range of shark

RISK TO HUMANS

The tiger shark's eating habits have earned it the

Tiger stripes

The tiger shark's stripes are most prominent when it is young. They gradually fade away as it grows older.

Daily dishes

Jellyfish, turtles, and dolphins are just a few of the animals in the tiger shark's natural diet.

Tiger shark teeth are curved, with lethal, jagged edges.

nickname "garbage can of the sea."

Thresher

One of the athletes of the shark world, the thresher often uses its long, thin tail to propel itself right out of the water.

PELAGIC THRESHER SHARK
Alopias pelagicus

ORDER
Mackerel sharks

BODY LENGTH
10 feet (3 m)

HABITAT

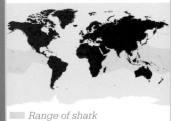

Range of shark

RISK TO HUMANS

Record breaker
The thresher's tail is longer than any other shark's. It uses it to round up schools of fish to eat.

Large pectoral (chest) fins work as stabilizers.

Shark tails Different tail fin shapes

You can tell a lot about a shark from its tail. The shape may determine how fast it can swim and how agile it is in the water.

porbeagle shark

gray nurse shark

cookie-cutter shark

The cookie-cutter uses its tail to rotate its body while biting flesh from its prey.

Pacific angel shark

tropical saw shark

Two keels on its tail help the porbeagle cut through water.

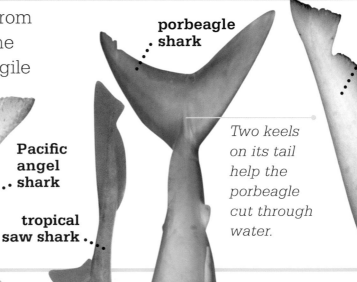

Endangered

Threshers have been overfished and are now listed as vulnerable.

Find out more about how sharks move on pages 16–17.

Bigeye threshers, like other sharks, are caught for their fins.

The tail is as long as the rest of the shark's body.

The whiplike tail can create underwater shock waves, stunning fish without touching them.

The tiger shark flexes its long upper tail fin to give it a burst of speed.

The zebra shark's long tail is perfect for cruising in shallow waters.

pelagic thresher shark

tiger shark

zebra shark

great white shark

Mako

The shortfin mako is a sleek predator known for its aggression and its record-breaking speed.

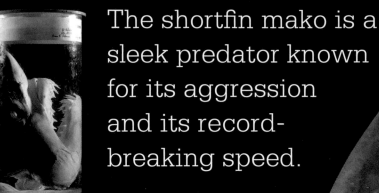

Telltale teeth

The mako's smooth-edged teeth are narrow and hooked. They are perfect for gripping the slippery fish that makos love to eat, such as herring and tuna.

SHORTFIN MAKO SHARK
Isurus oxyrinchus
ORDER Mackerel sharks
BODY LENGTH 10 feet (3 m)
HABITAT

■ *Range of shark*

RISK TO HUMANS

Makos attack from below, shooting upward at high speeds to surprise their prey above.

Top predators

Makos are top predators in the open ocean. Once they are fully grown, they have no enemies, other than humans.

Makos are incredible jumpers—they can leap

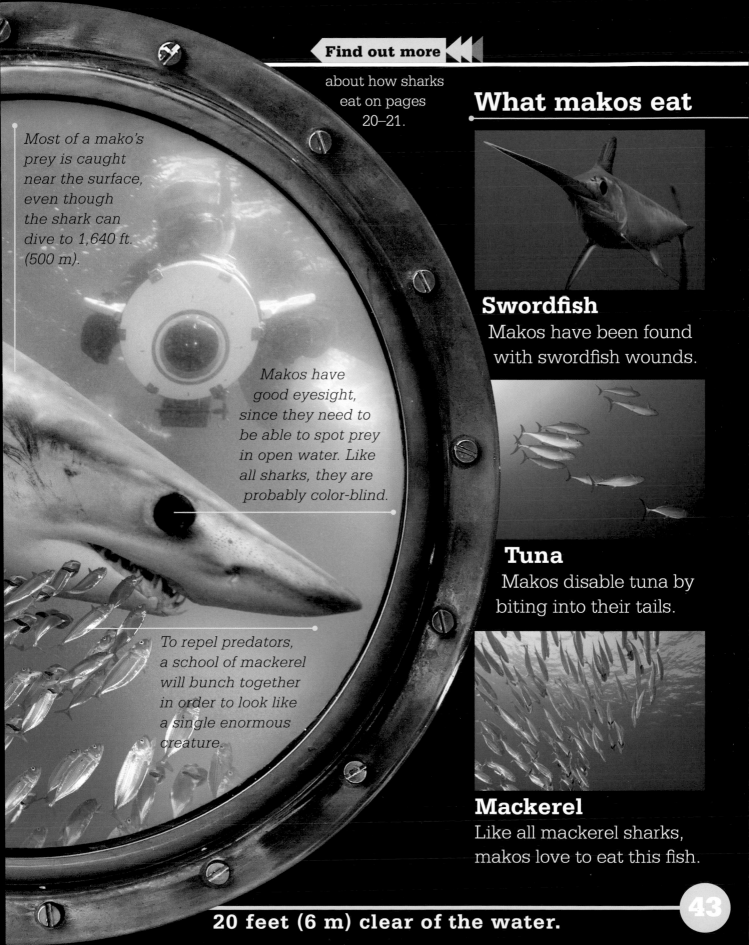

Find out more ◀◀◀

about how sharks
eat on pages
20–21.

What makos eat

*Most of a mako's
prey is caught
near the surface,
even though
the shark can
dive to 1,640 ft.
(500 m).*

*Makos have
good eyesight,
since they need to
be able to spot prey
in open water. Like
all sharks, they are
probably color-blind.*

*To repel predators,
a school of mackerel
will bunch together
in order to look like
a single enormous
creature.*

Swordfish
Makos have been found
with swordfish wounds.

Tuna
Makos disable tuna by
biting into their tails.

Mackerel
Like all mackerel sharks,
makos love to eat this fish.

20 feet (6 m) clear of the water.

Tagging and tracking

1 Shark research

Sharks are disappearing quickly. To help them, scientists need to know more about how they live. One way to study sharks is to track them.

2 Lured with food

Scientists at sea catch small sharks in nets. They capture large sharks with baited lines. Once a shark is caught, it is pulled over to the boat.

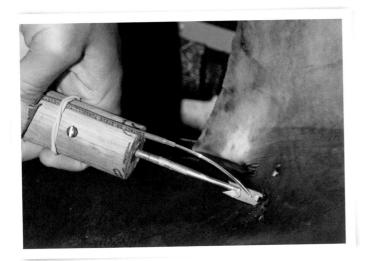

5 Attaching tags

An acoustic tag, which emits a coded pulse of sound, is attached to the base of the shark's dorsal fin using a tagging needle.

6 Release

Less than five minutes later, the shark is ready to be released. The sling is lowered back into the water, and the shark swims free.

Satellite tracking apps let you follow individual sharks

3 Out of the water

The shark is carefully maneuvered into a plastic sling, then hauled aboard. The team must work fast or the shark will suffocate.

4 Vital statistics

The shark's size, sex, and age are quickly measured, and a sample of its DNA is taken. It is now ready to be tagged.

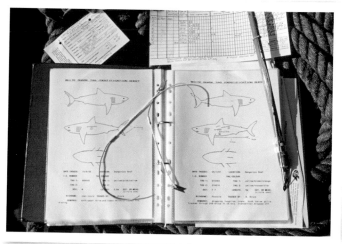

7 Keeping track

Hydrophones, or underwater microphones, pick up signals from tagged sharks, showing where they are. Other tags relay data to satellites.

8 On the record

Records of sightings of particular sharks at sea are kept in logbooks. Along with the data from tags, these build a picture of a shark's habits.

on your smartphone.

Amazing travelers

Some sharks travel across whole oceans. They migrate, or move to another area, in search of food, warmer waters, or a safe place to give birth.

Blue sharks

Some blue sharks make a 9,300-mile (15,000 km) round trip each year, from North American waters to near Europe, where they give birth to pups.

In the eastern Pacific, great whites migrate to feeding grounds that some call the "White Shark Café."

NORTH AMERICA

Bermuda

PACIFIC OCEAN

ATLANTIC OCEAN

SOUTH AMERICA

Epic journeys

Every year, ocean and land animals migrate incredible distances.

LONGEST INSECT MIGRATION:
monarch butterfly
2,880 miles (4,635 km)

LONGEST MAMMAL MIGRATION:
humpback whale
5,100 miles (8,200 km)

LONGEST BIRD MIGRATION:
Arctic tern
50,000 miles
(80,500 km)

LONGEST LAND-BASED ANIMAL MIGRATION:
Grant caribou
2,980 miles (4,800 km)

Tiger sharks

Some tiger sharks migrate when it gets cold. In summer, they live in open water near Bermuda. In the fall, they swim over 1,000 miles (1,600 km) south to warmer waters.

In 2009, a shiver (group) of over 400 whale sharks was

Bull sharks

Most of the world's sharks spend their lives at sea, but bull sharks are different. Pregnant females migrate to river mouths to give birth. Bull sharks also swim up rivers, eating fish and turtles and sometimes attacking humans.

A saltwater crocodile lunches on a bull shark on a riverbank in Australia.

EUROPE

ASIA

AFRICA

INDIAN OCEAN

AUSTRALIA

Great white sharks

Tagged adult great white sharks have been tracked traveling over 6,500 miles (10,500 km) between South Africa and Australia as they follow schools of fish.

THE GREAT WHITE SHARK "NICOLE" TRAVELED MORE THAN

13,670 MI. (22,000 KM)

FROM **AFRICA TO AUSTRALIA** AND BACK AGAIN IN 2004—THE LONGEST RECORDED SHARK JOURNEY.

seen looking for food off Mexico's Yucatán Peninsula.

Biggest of all

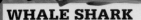

WHALE SHARK
Rhincodon typus

ORDER
Carpet sharks

LENGTH
up to 59 feet (18 m)

HABITAT

Range of shark

RISK TO HUMANS

The world's biggest sharks are harmless to humans. They feed on young fish and small drifting animals, filtering them from the sea.

The shark's tiny eyes look out on either side of its head.

Filter feeder

A whale shark sucks up huge mouthfuls of water, then filters it through its gill rakers. Small prey stay trapped in its mouth.

A whale shark's ridged back is marked like a checkerboard.

basking
shark

Other filter feeders

Second in size only to the whale shark, the basking shark lives mainly in cold-water regions. It cruises with its mouth open wide.

A whale shark's mouth can be up to 5 feet (1.5 m) wide.

Living giants

An adult whale shark is as long as a school bus. It weighs over 22 tons—that's heavier than a school bus full of passengers!

Whale sharks are the world's biggest fish.

Inshore sharks

Many sharks live near land, eating the plentiful food of coastal habitats. They usually ignore the people they share these waters with, but watch out for the deadly bull shark!

scoophead shark

copper shark

shark

tropical saw shark

lemon shark

gray reef shark

Atlantic sharpnose shark

gray nurse shark

zebra shark

blacktip shark

necklace
carpet shark

scalloped hammerhead shark

bull
shark

whitetip reef
shark

Pacific sharpnose shark

smooth
hammerhead
shark

broadnose sevengill
shark

bonnethead
shark

longnose saw shark

winghead shark

Gray reef

GRAY REEF SHARK

Carcharhinus amblyrhynchos

ORDER
Ground sharks

BODY LENGTH
8 feet (2.5 m)

HABITAT

■ *Range of shark*

RISK TO HUMANS

Dead end
These sharks herd fish prey against sharp coral so that they have no escape.

Ruler of its colorful coral kingdom, the gray reef shark patrols the water, watching for unwary prey.

Naturally curious, gray reef sharks will often swim up to divers. But watch out if a shark's body hunches into an S shape. It is feeling threatened and may attack.

Whitetip reef sharks often wriggle into crevices to catch prey.

gray reef shark

Whitetip reef

When darkness falls on the reef, whitetip reef sharks emerge from hidden caves and crevices to feed.

Rich reefs

These sharks love to snack on some of the 4,000 different kinds of delicious octopuses, crustaceans, and fish that live in coral reefs.

Taking a break

Whitetip reef sharks can pump water over their gills, so they don't have to keep swimming to breathe.

whitetip reef shark

WHITETIP REEF SHARK

Triaenodon obesus

ORDER
Ground sharks

BODY LENGTH
6.5 feet (2 m)

HABITAT

Range of shark

RISK TO HUMANS

Eyes shut!

A shark bite is potentially dangerous—even for the shark! As a blue shark closes in for the kill, its third eyelid closes automatically to keep the eye from being damaged during a big bite.

third eyelid

Sharks don't need to blink like humans do, since the

seawater keeps their eyes clean.

Hammerhead

An incredible winged head makes hammerheads easy to recognize. With an eye on each end of their heads, these sharks can scan for prey in all directions.

Visual weakness

Like all hammerheads, the bonnethead has a blind spot in front of its nose!

Unlike us, a hammerhead can see up and down at the same time.

eye

mouth

This is a smooth hammerhead shark as seen from below.

Hammerheads sometimes swim in schools of up to 100. At night, they often hunt alone.

Great shapes A shark's hammer form may vary.

Frilly edges
The scalloped hammerhead's hammer has rounded lobes. This shark eats stingrays, despite their toxic barbs.

Arched front
Found in shallow waters, the scoophead has a curved front edge on its hammer. It sometimes eats small sharks.

A smooth hammerhead scans the seabed for stingrays.

Hammer scanner
A hammerhead's head contains electrical sensors. The shark uses these sensors to scan the ocean floor for hidden prey.

SMOOTH HAMMERHEAD SHARK

Sphyrna zygaena

ORDER
Ground sharks

BODY LENGTH
13 feet (4 m)

HABITAT

Range of shark

RISK TO HUMANS

On the seabed

From flat-bodied wobbegongs to lumpy horn sharks, seabed sharks are colored and shaped to stay hidden on the ocean floor.

chain cat shark

Port Jackson shark

spotted wobbegong

leopard shark

sand devil

brown-banded bamboo shark

Galápagos bullhead shark

Indonesian speckled carpet shark

prickly
dogfish

tawny nurse shark

blind shark

angular
rough shark

gray
smooth-hound
shark

tope shark

cobbler
wobbegong

epaulette shark

angel shark

white-spotted
bamboo shark

ornate wobbegong

Wobbegong

Wobbegongs are sit-and-wait hunters, with incredible camouflage that matches the seabed. They can stay motionless for hours, until something swims close to their deadly jaws.

TASSELED WOBBEGONG

Eucrossorhinus dasypogon

ORDER
Carpet sharks

BODY LENGTH
4 feet (1.25 m)

HABITAT

■ *Range of shark*

RISK TO HUMANS

shaggy beard

The name *wobbegong* comes from an Australian

Wobbegongs love to eat fish, crabs, and octopuses. They can dislocate their jaws to swallow large prey.

Ambush hunters

There are 12 kinds of wobbegong, and all hunt by ambushing passersby. They will injure you if you step on them by mistake.

Jaws open wide for prey.

Can you see me?

A wobbegong can change color over several days to blend in with its background. Can you spot the sharks in these four pictures?

eye

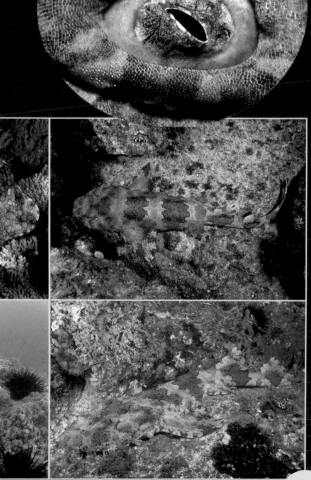

aboriginal language and means "shaggy beard."

Horn shark

Horn sharks feed on animals with hard shells. These sharks have flattened back teeth for crushing, and amazingly strong bites for their size.

HORN SHARK
Heterodontus francisci
ORDER Bullhead sharks
BODY LENGTH 3 feet (1 m)
HABITAT

■ *Range of shark*

RISK TO HUMANS

Defense
The horn shark is named for the sharp spike in front of its dorsal (upper or back) fins. This keeps many enemies from attacking it.

The spike, or horn, sticks in the tender flesh of a predator's mouth.

Starting life The horn shark's incredible eggs

① Spiral case
Horn sharks lay eggs in spiral cases. They jam the cases into crevices in the seabed.

② Hatching
Up to ten months later, a young horn shark is ready to hatch. It makes a tear in the case.

③ Pup
The young fish wriggles free. Sometimes the empty egg case will wash ashore.

Horn sharks "walk" across the seabed by shuffling

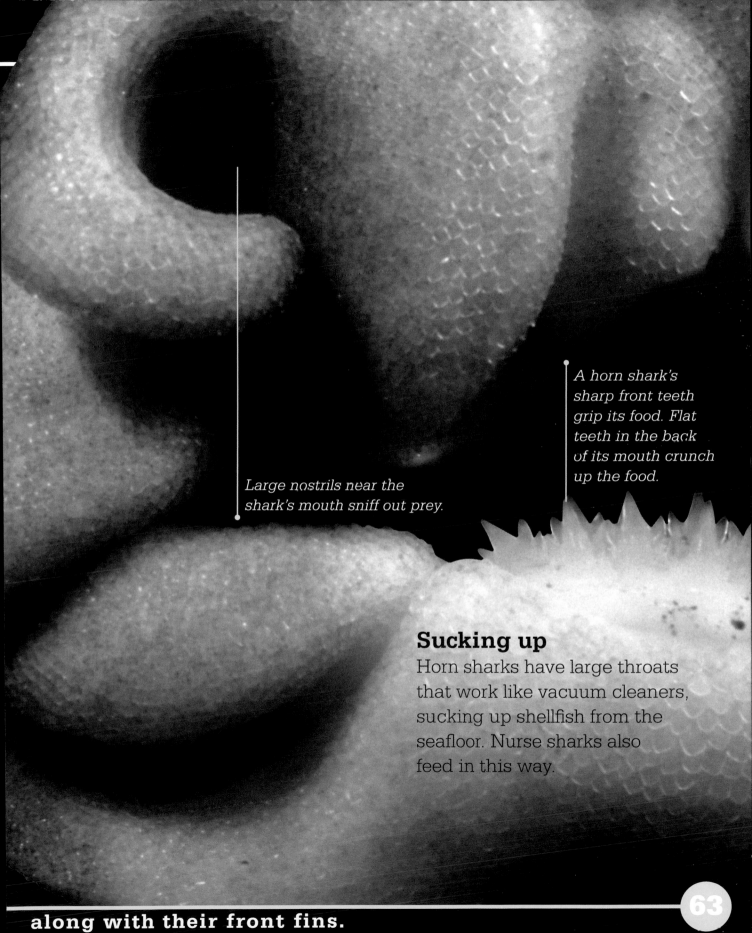

A horn shark's sharp front teeth grip its food. Flat teeth in the back of its mouth crunch up the food.

Large nostrils near the shark's mouth sniff out prey.

Sucking up

Horn sharks have large throats that work like vacuum cleaners, sucking up shellfish from the seafloor. Nurse sharks also feed in this way.

along with their front fins.

In the depths

In 1976, scientists discovered the first known megamouth shark. Since then, submersibles exploring the ocean's depths with cameras have found some of the strangest sharks of all.

Not such a sweet fish

The cookie-cutter shark lurks at depths of up to 11,500 feet (3,500 m) during the day but moves toward the surface at night. When feeding, it uses its lips to attach to prey, then spins around, cutting out a piece of flesh with its teeth.

Unlike other sharks, a cookie-cutter replaces its whole lower set of teeth at the same time.

Sharks in the dark   Adapting to deep-sea life

Exploring the deep

Only robotic submersibles have been able to reach the incredible depths at which some sharks live. Here are a few that they have spotted.

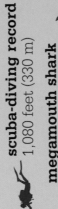

scuba-diving record
1,080 feet (330 m)

megamouth shark
1,950 feet (595 m)

sperm whale
3,280 feet
(1,000 m)

goblin shark
4,265 feet
(1,300 m)

frilled shark
4,200 feet
(1,280 m)

longnose cat shark
6,200 feet (1,890 m)

Pacific sleeper shark
6,560 feet (2,000 m)

Greenland shark
7,220 feet
(2,200 m)

bluntnose sixgill shark
8,200 feet
(2,500 m)

9,800 feet (3,000 m)

cookie-cutter shark
11,500 feet (3,500 m)

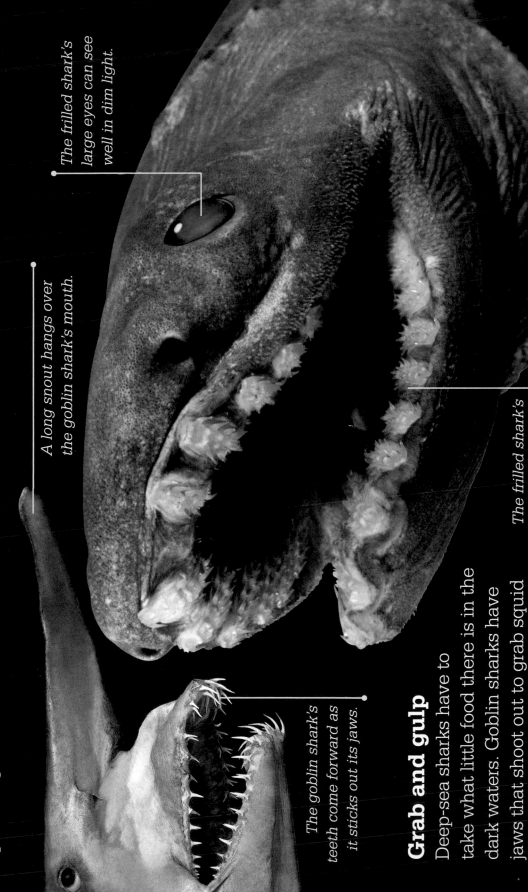

Portuguese dogfish
12,100 feet (3,675 m)

13,000 feet (4,000 m)

There is very little food for sharks to eat below this depth.

The frilled shark's large eyes can see well in dim light.

A long snout hangs over the goblin shark's mouth.

The frilled shark's teeth act like hooks to grip prey.

The goblin shark's teeth come forward as it sticks out its jaws.

Goblin hunting

In the inky blackness, goblin sharks hunt by sensing prey with special organs in their snouts.

Glowing giant

The megamouth shark attracts the jellyfish and plankton it feeds on with its reflective lips.

Grab and gulp

Deep-sea sharks have to take what little food there is in the dark waters. Goblin sharks have jaws that shoot out to grab squid and fish. Frilled sharks open their mouths extra wide to eat prey.

Living with **sharks**

Many people are afraid of sharks, even though attacks on humans are very rare. Sharks are the ones really in trouble: Over 100,000 are killed every day, and some species may soon become extinct.

Myths and legends

Seafaring people have always feared and respected sharks. Over the centuries, many myths and legends have grown up around these unpredictable predators.

Samebito

Legend of Samebito

In Japanese myths, Samebito is half man and half shark. His tears turn into 10,000 precious stones.

The word *shark* may come from *xoc*, a word used by

Star sign

The Warao Indians of South America think that the stars in the constellation we call Orion form the leg of a man. This man tried to train a shark to kill his mother-in-law, but her daughter cut off his leg instead.

Orion Nebula

A new look Sharks are still feared and revered today.

Airborne sharks
In World War II, shark faces were sometimes painted on the noses of fighter planes.

Movie stars
Recently, sharks have been box-office hits in movies such as *Shark Tale* (2004).

Fin of fear
A shark's dorsal fin poking above the water is a terrifying symbol in contemporary culture.

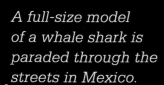

A full-size model of a whale shark is paraded through the streets in Mexico.

Festivals
Shark festivals are common in some parts of the world. The massive whale shark (see pages 48–49) is often one of the top stars.

the ancient Maya of Central America.

Under threat

Every year, at least 40 million sharks are killed. Some die accidentally, but most are deliberately caught by people for food or for fun.

Shark finning

For fishermen, the most valuable parts of a shark are its fins. These are cut off, dried, and sold to make shark fin soup. The rest of the shark is often thrown away.

Great white sharks are now as rare as tigers. Only about

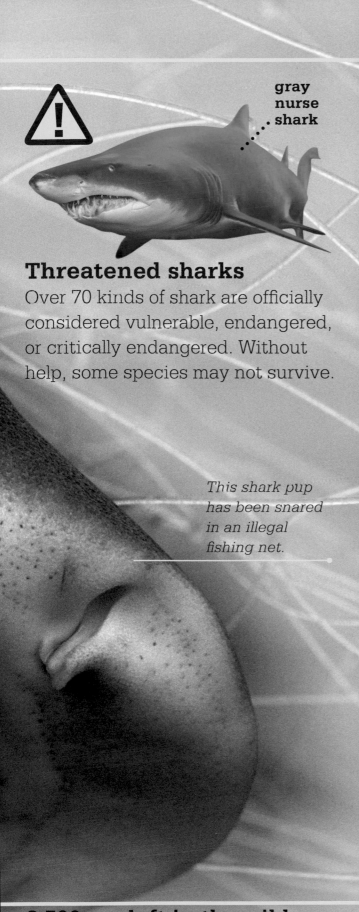

gray
nurse
shark

Threatened sharks

Over 70 kinds of shark are officially considered vulnerable, endangered, or critically endangered. Without help, some species may not survive.

This shark pup has been snared in an illegal fishing net.

3,500 are left in the wild.

Changing the balance

Sharks are part of food chains. If we kill sharks, other animals may suffer.

Reef shark

Many reef sharks are killed per year. Reef sharks eat fish, like groupers.

Grouper

Fewer reef sharks means a bigger population of groupers.

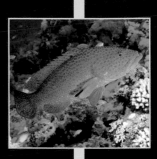

Reef lobster

More groupers means that more of their prey, reef lobsters, are eaten.

Sea slug

Fewer reef lobsters means a bigger population of their prey, sea slugs.

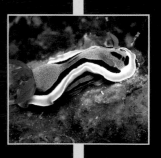

Coral polyp

Sea slugs eat coral polyps. More sea slugs means coral reefs will decline.

What you can do . . .

1 Join!
Join an organization that defends sharks, such as the Shark Alliance or Shark Savers. They work to save sharks all over the world.

2 Be a shark champion
Explain to your classmates why sharks are important, and why we need to keep them in the seas. Stand up for sharks!

5 Say no to plastic
Use less plastic packaging and fewer plastic shopping bags. Plastic can kill sharks if it gets washed into the sea.

6 Visit an aquarium
Big aquariums are great places to come face-to-face with sharks and their close relatives skates and rays. So pop in and say hello!

With your help, sharks will continue to roam the

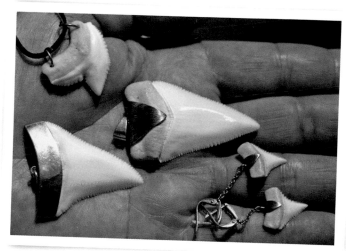

3 Watch what you eat

Refuse to eat shark fin soup. Also, watch out for menu items like rock salmon, which is actually shark meat in disguise.

4 Watch what you buy

Don't buy shark-tooth jewelry or dried shark jaws. Steer clear of creams and cosmetics that contain shark-liver oil (sometimes listed as squalene).

7 Find out more

Discover more about sharks in other books and on TV. Learn to surf safely for information about our fishy friends on the Internet.

8 Start a shark file

Keep a record of all the sharks that you learn about, including ones in the news. You'll soon have your own up-to-date shark file.

oceans, just as they have for millions of years.

Interview with a marine

Name: Mark Spalding
Profession: Coral reef and mangrove forest expert for the Nature Conservancy

Q **When did you become interested in the ocean?**

A It was probably from playing in rock pools as a very young child. I first saw a coral reef when I was 11 and that was it—I was hooked.

Q **How did you become a marine biologist?**

A I studied zoology [animals] and biogeography [life on Earth] at Cambridge University [UK]. I also got experience helping other researchers around the world.

Q **When did you first study sharks?**

A I went on a scientific diving expedition to an isolated group of islands in the Indian Ocean. We found that the number of reef sharks had dropped drastically during the previous 20 years.

Q **What do you wear when you are diving?**

A On coral reefs, sharks are never really a threat, so just my usual outfit—a wet suit.

biologist

Q **How does it feel to swim close to a shark?**

A Breathtaking! They feel powerful as they cruise past. Their eyes seem to look right through you.

Q **Have you ever been bitten by a shark?**

A All sharks need respect, but very few are seriously dangerous. I've never come close to being bitten.

Q **Where is the best place for watching sharks?**

A Sadly, it's probably an aquarium. If you're able to, you can see wild sharks easily in Australia, the Bahamas, the Maldives, and Fiji.

Q **Have you ever met a rare shark relative?**

A I once worked in a remote river in Australia. I swam with turtles, crocodiles, and stingrays every day. I also saw two sawfish— these are close relatives of sharks and rays, and really, really rare.

Q **Why are sharks important?**

A Sharks are right at the top of the food chain. They keep down the number of smaller predators and allow other fish and invertebrates to flourish, helping diversity.

Q **Why are shark numbers falling?**

A They are being overfished. The greatest demand is for their fins. Sharks all over the world are being caught and their fins used to make shark fin soup.

Q **How can we protect sharks in the future?**

A We need to stop the fishing, but that probably also means trying to discourage people from eating sharks and shark fin soup.

Glossary

aquarium
A place where visitors can see different kinds of ocean creatures, such as dolphins and sharks.

bait ball
A school of fish that has been herded into the shape of a ball.

camouflage
Natural coloring that helps animals blend in with their surroundings.

cartilage
A strong, flexible material that shark skeletons are made of.

coral
An underwater substance made up of the skeletons of tiny sea creatures.

coral reef
A reef made of coral and other materials that have solidified into rock.

countershading
A kind of camouflage that hides sharks from above and below.

crevice
A narrow opening in, for example, a coral reef.

crustacean
An animal with a hard outer skeleton, such as a lobster or crab.

DNA
A chemical found in all living things. It contains the instructions needed to build a body and make it work.

dorsal fin
An upright fin on a shark's back. Most sharks have two dorsal fins; the one in front is usually bigger.

embryo
A very young animal, not yet born, in the early stages of development.

endangered species
A plant or animal that is at risk of dying out, usually because of human activity.

extinct
No longer in existence, having died out.

This reef shark, seen from below, is cruising off the Great Barrier Reef in Australia.

filter feeder
An animal that eats by filtering food from the water.

food chain
A series of living things that depend on one another for food. Each plant or animal is a link in the chain.

fossil
The remains of an ancient animal or plant, preserved in some way, such as in rock.

gill
One of a pair of organs near a fish's mouth, through which it draws oxygen from water.

habitat
The place where an animal or plant usually lives and finds its food.

hydrophone
A microphone that picks up underwater sounds.

fin
A thin, flat body part on a fish that is used for moving and steering through water.

invertebrate
An animal with no backbone, such as an octopus or squid.

migrate
To travel a long distance to breed or to feed.

pectoral fin
One of pair of fins at the front of a shark's body, just behind its head.

predator
An animal that hunts other animals for food.

prey
An animal that is hunted by another animal as food.

reef
A strip of rock or coral near the ocean's surface.

scale
One of many hard, tiny overlapping plates that cover a shark's body.

school
A group of fish that swim and feed together.

streamlined
Shaped to slip easily through water or air.

toxic
Poisonous to living things.

Index

Thank you

Photography

1, 2–3 (background): iStockphoto; 2br, 3tr: Marine Themes Pty Ltd; 4–5 (background): iStockphoto; 4 (shark): Martin Strmko/iStockphoto; 5 (shark): David Fleetham/Visuals Unlimited, Inc./Photo Researchers, Inc.; 5 (coral): iStockphoto; 6–7: Gary Bell/OceanwideImages.com; 8–9: Andy Murch/Visuals Unlimited, Inc./Science Photo Library; 8tr: iStockphoto; 9tr: Michael Patrick O'Neill/Photo Researchers, Inc.; 9cr, 9bl: Marine Themes Pty Ltd; 9br: Ian Scott/iStockphoto; 10–11 (water background): iStockphoto; 10–11 (sand background): Dirk-jan Mattaar/Dreamstime; 10–11 (columns): Stocksnapper/Dreamstime; 10 (whale shark): Krzysztof Odziomek/Dreamstime; 11 (great white shark): iStockphoto; 11 (nurse shark): Kjersti Joergensen/Dreamstime; 10–11 (all others): Marine Themes Pty Ltd; 12 (elephant fish): Bill Boyle/OceanwideImages.com; 12 (rabbitfish): public domain; 12–13 (all others): Marine Themes Pty Ltd; 14–15 (background): iStockphoto; 14tl: Christian Darkin/Photo Researchers, Inc.; 14bl: iStockphoto; 14–15c: image produced by Karen Karr for the Virginia Museum of Natural History, image used courtesy of VMNH; 15tr: Ashok Rodrigues/iStockphoto; 15c, 15b: Christian Darkin/Photo Researchers, Inc.; 16–17c: iStockphoto; 16bl: Eye of Science/Photo Researchers, Inc.; 16bcl: iStockphoto; 16bcr: Anankkml/Dreamstime; 16br: iStockphoto; 17tl: Alexis Rosenfeld/Science Photo Library/Photo Researchers, Inc.; 17bl: iStockphoto; 17bc: David Fleetham/Visuals Unlimited, Inc.; 17br: SeaPics.com; 18–19: Marine Themes Pty Ltd; 18bc, 18br, 19bl, 19bc, 19br: iStockphoto; 20cl: Animals Animals/SuperStock; 20bl: iStockphoto; 20 (teeth): Rowan Byrne/SeaPics.com; 20 (great white shark jaw, prickly dogfish jaw): Marine Themes Pty Ltd; 20–21t: Doug Perrine/SeaPics.com; 21cl: Marine Themes Pty Ltd; 21r: SeaPics.com; 22–23: Naluphoto/Dreamstime; 24–25 (shark birth): SeaPics.com; 24–25 (egg cases): Marine Themes Pty Ltd; 25c: Alex Kerstitch/Visuals Unlimited/Science Photo Library; 25tr: Marine Themes Pty Ltd; 25br: Jeff Rotman/Nature Picture Library; 26–27 (background): ryan burke/iStockphoto; 26–27 (frames): Iakov Filimonov/Shutterstock; 26tr: Marine Themes Pty Ltd; 26tl: WaterFrame/Alamy; 26cl: Roberto Nistri/Alamy; 26bl: Fiona Ayerst/Dreamstime; 26–27b: Scubazoo/Science Photo Library; 27tl: Photomyeye/Dreamstime; 27tr, 27cr, 27br: Marine Themes Pty Ltd; 28–29: Alberto Pomares/iStockphoto; 30 (dusky shark): OceanwideImages.com; 30 (crocodile shark), 31 (cookie-cutter shark): public domain; 31 (great white shark): Willtu/Dreamstime; 31 (blue shark): Fiona Ayerst/Dreamstime; 30–31 (all others): Marine Themes Pty Ltd; 32–33: Stephen Frink Collection/Alamy; 32cl: Chris Dascher/iStockphoto; 32bl (map): pop_jop/iStockphoto; 32bl (shark icon): ryan burke/iStockphoto; 32tr: Terry Goss/Wikimedia Commons; 33cl: Moviestore Collection Ltd/Alamy; 33tr: Puddingpie/Dreamstime; 33rct: Kevin Browne/Alamy; 33rcb: SeaPics.com; 33br: Marine Themes Pty Ltd; 34–35: Steve Bloom Images/Alamy; 36tr: John_Woodcock/iStockphoto; 36c: Noah Hamilton Photography; 36bl: v0lha/iStockphoto; 37tl: Dejan Sarman/Dreamstime; 37tc: Marine Themes Pty Ltd; 37tr: Amanda Cotton/iStockphoto; 37bl: Noah Hamilton Photography; 38cl: Naluphoto/Dreamstime; 38–39 (jaws): Masa Ushioda/SeaPics.com; 38 (armor): Iakov Filimonov/Dreamstime; 38 (license plate): Michelle/Fotolia; 38 (antlers): joppo/Fotolia; 38 (horse): Alexia Khruscheva/Dreamstime; 38 (drum): Grafvision/Fotolia; 38 (gas can): Alexandr Vlassyuk/Fotolia; 38 (dynamite): Ongap/Dreamstime; 39 (seagull): F9photos/Dreamstime; 39 (squid): Wksp/Dreamstime; 39 (jellyfish): Dwight Smith/Dreamstime; 39 (turtle): Idreamphotos/Dreamstime; 39 (dolphin): Duncan Noakes/Dreamstime; 39 (lobster): Maceofoto/Dreamstime; 39tr: Chris Butler/Photo Researchers, Inc.; 39br, 40–41c: Marine Themes Pty Ltd; 40 (cookie-cutter shark): Roberto Nistri/Alamy; 40 (all others): Marine Themes Pty Ltd; 41tl: Steffen Foerster/Shutterstock; 41 (tiger shark): SeaPics.com; 41 (great white shark): Marine Themes Pty Ltd; 41 (zebra shark): Zeamonkeyimages/Dreamstime; 41 (pelagic thresher shark): Marine Themes Pty Ltd; 42tl: Natural History Museum, London/Photo Researchers, Inc.; 42cl: Marine Themes Pty Ltd; 42–43 (porthole): Leon Suharevsky/iStockphoto; 42–43 (shark and diver): Marine Themes Pty Ltd; 42–43 (mackerel): stephan kerkhofs/iStockphoto; 43tr: Angel Fitor/Science Photo Library; 43cr: Richard Carey/iStockphoto; 43br: stephan kerkhofs/iStockphoto; 44tl: Fiona Ayerst/iStockphoto; 44tr, 44bl, 44br, 45tl, 45tr: Marine

Themes Pty Ltd; 45bl: Louise Murray/Science Photo Library; 45br: Jeff Rotman/Photo Researchers, Inc.; 46–47 (map): Etunya/Dreamstime; 46tc: Marine Themes Pty Ltd; 46 (monarch butterfly): Jordan McCullough/iStockphoto; 46 (Arctic tern): alarifoto/iStockphoto; 46bc: Naluphoto/Dreamstime; 47tr: Newspix/News Ltd/3rd Party Managed Reproduction & Supply Rights; 47cr: Jagronick/Dreamstime; 48tl: J. Henning Buchholz/Dreamstime; 48–49c: Jamiegodson/Dreamstime; 48–49 (water flea): Laguna Design/Photo Researchers, Inc.; 48–49 (all other small prey): D.P. Wilson/FLPA/Photo Researchers, Inc.; 49tc: Alex Mustard/Nature Picture Library; 49bc (bus): Scholastic; 50 (scoophead shark): SeaPics.com; 50–51 (scalloped hammerhead shark): Steve Bloom Images/Alamy; 50–51 (zebra shark): Zeamonkeyimages/Dreamstime; 50–51 (longnose saw shark): OceanwideImages.com; 51 (whitetip reef shark): Olga Khoroshunova/Dreamstime; 51 (bonnethead shark): Doug Perrine/SeaPics.com; 51 (winghead shark): Stephen Kajiura/SeaPics.com; 50–51 (all others): Marine Themes Pty Ltd; 52tl: Carol Buchanan/Dreamstime; 52tc: Alexis Rosenfeld/Photo Researchers, Inc.; 52c (shark): Martin Strmko/iStockphoto; 52cl (school of fish): Paul Vinten/iStockphoto; 52bl (eel): Richard Carey/iStockphoto; 52bc (angelfish): cynoclub/iStockphoto; 52–53 (red sponge): Richard Carey/iStockphoto; 52–53 (background): Igor Borisov/iStockphoto; 53tc: Marine Themes Pty Ltd; 53tr: Sburel/Dreamstime; 53bc (shark): David Fleetham/Visuals Unlimited, Inc.; 53bl (school of fish): Richard Carey/iStockphoto; 54–55: Marine Themes Pty Ltd; 56–57 (background and shark c): stockfoto/Fotolia; 56tl: J Hindman/Fotolia; 56b (shark): Marine Themes Pty Ltd; 56b (background): Logorilla/iStockphoto; 57tr: Dream69/Dreamstime; 57 (scalloped hammerhead): Mark Doherty/Fotolia; 57 (scoophead): OceanwideImages.com; 57 (smooth hammerhead l, smooth hammerhead r): Marine Themes Pty Ltd; 57bl: Richard Carey/Fotolia; 58 (sand devil): Chris Moncrieff/Dreamstime; 59 (angular rough shark): Citron/Wikimedia Commons; 59 (tawny nurse shark): sdubrov/Fotolia; 58–59 (all others), 60tl: Marine Themes Pty Ltd; 60–61b: Andy Murch/Visuals Unlimited/Science Picture Library; 61tl: Jamiegodson/Dreamstime; 61tr: Marine Themes Pty Ltd; 61crt: OceanwideImages.com; 61clb: Teguh Tirtaputra/Dreamstime; 61crb, 61bl, 61br, 62tl, 62c, 62bl: Marine Themes Pty Ltd; 62bc: Stephen Frink Collection/Alamy; 62br: Phillip Colla/SeaPics.com; 63: Stephen Frink Collection/Alamy; 64 (background): Misko Kordic/Dreamstime; 64 (cookie-cutter shark): Bill Curtsinger/Getty Images; 64 (goblin shark): e-Photography/Makoto Hirose/SeaPics.com; 64 (megamouth shark): Bruce Rasner/Rotman/Nature Picture Library; 64 (scuba icon): Tulay Over/iStockphoto; 64 (whale icon): Ace_Create/iStockphoto; 65 (goblin shark): David Shen/SeaPics.com; 65 (frilled shark): Marine Themes Pty Ltd; 66–67: Uwe Zucchi/AFP/Getty Images; 68: The Stapleton Collection/Bridgeman; 69tr: pixbox77/Fotolia; 69cl: Ivan Cholakov/Shutterstock; 69cm: DreamWorks Animation/Bureau L.A. Collection/Corbis; 69cr: Strezhnev Pavel/Fotolia; 69bc: John S. Vater, Ceviche Tours, www.cevichetours.com; 70–71: Tui De Roy/Getty Images; 70cl, 71tl: Marine Themes Pty Ltd; 71tr: Carol Buchanan/Dreamstime; 71crt: Mark Doherty/Dreamstime; 71crm: Marine Themes Pty Ltd; 71crb: Andamanse/Dreamstime; 71br: Bkaiser/Dreamstime; 72tl: Song Zhenping/Xinhua Press/Corbis; 72tr: Tova Bornovski/Micronesian Shark Foundation; 72bl: Alexis Rosenfeld/Photo Researchers, Inc.; 72br: Hbh/Dreamstime; 73tl: Agustua Fajarmon/Dreamstime; 73tr: Jeffrey L. Rotman/Getty Images; 73bl: Monkey Business Images/Dreamstime; 73br: July Store/Shutterstock; 74tr: Mark Spalding/The Nature Conservancy; 74bl: Predrag Vuckovic/iStockphoto; 74–75b (background): Tobias Helbig/iStockphoto; 74b (shark): Chris Dascher/iStockphoto; 75tr: Thinkstock; 76–77 (porthole): Leon Suharevsky/iStockphoto; 76–77 (shark): Stevenmaltby/Dreamstime; 78–79: Pinosub/Shutterstock; 80: Aaron Croft/iStockphoto.

Cover

Background: George Toubalis/Shutterstock. Front cover: (tl) Marine Themes Pty Ltd; (c) Mike Parry/Minden Pictures; (bl) Ian Scott/Dreamstime; (br) Ralf Kraft/Dreamstime. Spine: camellia/Shutterstock. Back cover: (tr) OceanwideImages.com; (computer monitor) Manaemedia/Dreamstime.